P9-DUD-428

Girls Think of Everything

Stories of Ingenious Inventions by Women

Catherine Thimmesh

Illustrated by Melissa Sweet

HOUGHTON MIFFLIN COMPANY BOSTON 2000

Text copyright © 2000 by Catherine Thimmesh
Illustrations copyright © 2000 by Melissa Sweet

All rights reserved. For information about permission to reproduce selections from this book,
write to Permissions, Houghton Mifflin Company, 215 Park Avenue South, New York, New York 10003.

Kevlar® is a registered trademark of Du Pont.
Liquid Paper® is a registered trademark of The Gillette Company.
Scotchgard™ is a trademark of 3M.
Snugli® is a registered trademark of Snugli, Incorporated.
Oops! Proof™ is a trademark of Little Kids, Incorporated.

The text of this book is set in 14-point Fairfield.
The illustrations are mixed media.
Collages photographed by Hugh Brantner Photography

Library of Congress Cataloging-in-Publication Data
Thimmesh, Catherine.
Girls think of everything: stories of ingenious inventions by women / by Catherine Thimmesh ;
illustrated by Melissa Sweet.
p.   cm.
Summary: Tells the story of how women throughout the ages have responded to situations confronting
them in daily life by inventing such items as correction fluid, space helmets, and disposable diapers.
ISBN 0-395-93744-2
1. Women inventors—United States—Biography—Juvenile literature. 2. Inventions—United States—
History—Juvenile literature. [1. Inventors. 2. Inventions. 3. Women Biography.] I. Sweet, Melissa, ill.
II. Title
T39.T48   2000
609.2'273 — dc21   [B]   99-36270   CIP

Printed in Singapore
TWP 10 9 8 7 6 5 4 3 2 1

1887   Anna Connelly   *fire escape*

1888   Miriam E. Benjamin   *"gong and signal chair"*

1889   Anna Breadin   *school desk*

1891   Annie Chilton   *house detacher*

1892   Harriet R. Tracy   *"lock and chain stitch" for sewing machine*

1892   Cynthia Westover   *street-cleaning cart*

1892   Leonie Callmeyer   *means for detecting the opening of sealed envelopes*

1892   Anna Mangin   *pastry fork*

1899   Letitia Geer   *medical syringes*

1902   Mary Anderson   *windshield wiper*

1904   Anonymous   *ice cream cone*

1904   Catherine Ryan   *Nut and Bolt lock for railroad tracks*

1905   Madam C. J. Walker   *hair-care products*

1908   Melitta Bentz   *drip coffee machine*

1912   Carrie B. Averill   *baby carrier*

1913   Rose O'Neill   *the Kewpie Doll*

1914   Mary P. Jacobs   *brassiere*

1915   Laura M. Hicks   *washmit*

1916   Madeline Turner   *fruit press*

1917   May Conner   *combined egg beater and potato masher*

1917   Ida Forbes   *electric hot water heater*

1918   Julie Auerbach   *detachable, self-adjusting corset strap*

1924   Elizabeth Phillips   *The Landlord's Game (early version of Monopoly™)*

1928   Marjorie Stewart Joyner   *permanent wave machine*

1930   Ruth Wakefield   *chocolate chip cookie*

1938   Katherine Burr Blodgett   *nonreflecting glass ("invisible" glass)*

1938   Gladys Whitcomb Geissmann   *glove construction*

1942   Hedwig Kiesler Maukey (also known as movie star Hedy Lamarr) and George Antheil
        secret communication system using "frequency hopping"

1943   Henrietta Mahim Bradberry   *bed rack to freshen clothes*

For Jaimie and Simon,
who invent new ways to amuse me every day.
—C.T.

batteries
go into
pocket

Jamie's
electric
skirt

In memory of Jamien Morehouse,
who invented many wonderful things.
—M.S.

In the beginning . . .

With a push you are free—bursting into the world scrunched up and screaming. "It's a girl!" the doctor announces. Or "It's a boy!" And so your life began. And with those very first breaths, and in those very first moments, your health and

well-being were evaluated through the eyes of an ingenious inventor: Dr. Virginia Apgar. Dr. Apgar developed the Newborn Scoring System—or Apgar Score—to measure five crucial aspects of a baby's health: color, pulse, reflexes, activity, and respiration. She recognized the urgency of identifying those newborns in need of emergency attention, and because of her innovation, hundreds of thousands of lives have been saved. Today, all medical professionals evaluate a new baby using the Apgar Score within minutes of birth. Right from the get-go, a woman's inventiveness and ingenuity touched your life. But that was only the beginning.

Whether in medicine or science, household products or high-tech gadgets, women invent—and their inventions surround us and affect our everyday lives. They have created cancer-fighting drugs, space helmets, coffeemakers, and disposable diapers. Women have invented games and toys and computer software programs.

"At first people refuse to believe that a strange new thing can be done, then they begin to hope it can be done, then they see it can be done— then it is done and all the world wonders why it was not done centuries ago."

—Frances Hodgson Burnett, author of The Secret Garden

Inventors create for a variety of reasons. Maybe you've heard the phrase "Necessity is the mother of invention"? It's true. An inventor sees a need and seeks to fill it. A long time ago, before there were record keepers or materials to keep records on, people went about their daily lives. And in doing so, they invented. According to oral tradition, as well as observations and studies conducted by anthropologists, women were responsible for some of the most fundamental and enduring innovations of all time. Because of their responsibilities within their families and communities, it appears that women

In the year 3000 B.C., the fourteen-year-old Chinese empress Hsi-ling-shi is credited with the discovery of silk. Silk is one of the oldest known textile fabrics, and for thirty centuries the method of gathering and weaving silk was a secret known only to the Chinese.

were the first to invent tools and utensils—including the mortar (a heavy bowl) and pestle (a clublike hammer) to prepare food, such as flour, and botanical medicines. They spun cotton together with flax, thereby inventing cloth. And they created the first shelters by designing and constructing huts and wigwams. It is said that women were the first to discover dyes to color cloth and tanning methods to make leather goods.

But many inventions evolve out of general curiosity—a sense of interest, a sense of "wouldn't it be fun if?" And then, of course, there are the accidents. The mistakes and happenstances that someone notices and develops. Take the ice-cream cone, for example. As the story goes, one day in 1904 at the World's Fair in St. Louis, Missouri, a young lady (whose name remains a mystery) struggled to eat her ice-cream sandwich and carry a bouquet of flowers. So she took the top cookie and wrapped it around the flowers, creating an impromptu vase. She then wrapped the remaining cookie around the ice cream so it wouldn't drip on her dress, and, there it was—the very first ice-cream cone. An ice-cream vendor who had run out of bowls witnessed her ingenuity and was soon selling ice-cream cones to eager passersby.

Throughout history, women have always been innovators. But their accomplishments have often been downplayed, skimmed over, or ignored altogether. In the year 1715, we have the first documented evidence of an invention by an American woman: a new method for cleaning and curing corn. Sybilla Masters had observed Native American women using heavy pestles to pound corn by hand, and she was determined to find a power-driven method. She was convinced such a process would be easier and more efficient than the usual practice of grinding the corn between two millstones.

Because America was still a British colony, Sybilla went to England to obtain a patent for her invention. Unfortunately, at that time, women were not allowed patents in their own names. In fact, women did not legally own any property whatsoever and were themselves considered to be the property of their husbands. So, for Sybilla to protect her invention, she had to settle for obtaining the patent in the name of her husband, Thomas Masters.

The patent awarded to Thomas read in part: "a new invention found out by Sybilla, his wife, for cleaning and curing the Indian Corn growing in the several colonies in America."

Nearly one hundred years would pass before an American woman's invention would legally be recognized as her own. Mary Dixon Kies has the honor of holding the first U.S. patent ever awarded to a woman in her own name. Mary created an innovative process of weaving straw with silk or thread, primarily for use in ladies' bonnets.

Mary was awarded a patent in 1809—just as straw bonnets were becoming extremely fashionable. Her invention alone heightened the New England hat

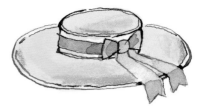

business, which in turn boosted the region's overall economy.

Against the odds, women have invented. They succeeded when many thought they'd fail. Madam C. J. Walker—the daughter of former slaves—invented hair care products for African-American women and a new method for selling them. She was born Sarah Breedlove, was orphaned at the age of seven,

The timing of Mary's invention proved to be lucky. The American government had just placed an embargo on European imports. No products from Europe could be shipped to America. With less competition, Mary enjoyed a tremendous demand for her hats.

married at fourteen, and widowed at twenty. For nearly twenty years she labored doing other people's laundry. Madam Walker began her business with a single product, a lot of confidence, and $1.50. She went door-to-door giving free demonstrations and showing before-and-after photos of herself. Within seven years, she had several hair care products and a thriving business. Madam C. J. Walker went on to become the first American woman self-made millionaire.

Today, in living rooms and labs, women are inventing. They are combining

A'Lelia Bundles/Madam Walker Family Collection

their curiosity and creativity with persistence and optimism. They are imagining. They are thinking and talking. "What if?" they ask. "How about?" they wonder. "Ah-ha!" they exclaim.

And gradually their ingenuity emerges. An inventiveness that touches all our lives, and perhaps energizes our own creativity—women and men, girls and boys alike. These are a few of their stories.

Ruth Wakefield
Chocolate Chip Cookies

The horses were tired; they were hungry. Time to grab a bite on the journey from Boston to New Bedford: a little hay, maybe some oats. After all, the busy Toll House on Route 18 in Whitman, Massachusetts, was a rest stop for horses. But in time, that would all change. Hay and oats would give way to salads and soups and chicken in white sauce. And, as luck would have it, chocolate chip cookies.

It was an accident. A simple mistake. A last-minute effort to save time. A just-toss-it-in-and-it-will-all-work-out sort of gesture that led to Ruth Wakefield's creation of the crunchy, chewy, oh-so-delicious chocolate chip cookie. Her invention is one of the most enduring, one of the most duplicated, and one of the most loved creations ever.

Ruth's restaurant was relatively new. She and her husband had taken the old Toll House and converted it into a dining establishment—the Toll House Inn— serving people this time, not horses. Early on, it was small, with space to seat thirty. As co-owner, manager, hostess, and cook, Ruth kept very busy. One day in 1930, she was making a batch of chocolate-butter drop cookies, popular at the time. The recipe required her to melt chocolate squares and pour the chocolate into the batter before baking.

Instead, because she was in a hurry, she simply broke the chocolate into chunks, tossed them in

COOKIES

PIES

BISCUITS

FROSTINGS

JELLIES

CANDIES

Ruth Wakefield's Toll House Cookies

Bake 10-12 minutes at 375°   Makes 100 cookies

Cream
1 cup butter, add
3/4 c. brown sugar and
2 eggs beaten. Dissolve
1 tsp. baking soda in
1 tsp. hot water, and mix in
2 1/4 c. flour sifted with
1 tsp. salt. Lastly add

1 c. chopped nuts and
2 bars Nestle's yellow label
chocolate, semisweet, cut
into pieces the size of a pea.
Flavor with
1 tsp. vanilla extract
Drop in half teaspoons on
greased cookie sheet.

4	"	(2 pints)	
4	"	of sifted flour	
2	"	" butter	
1/2	cup	"	
2	cups	" granulated sugar	
2 1/2	"	" powdered sugar	
1	pint	" water or milk	
1	"	" solid fat	
4		tablespoons of coffee	
2	"	" butter	
2	"	" sugar	
4		" flour	

Today's multimillion-dollar chocolate chip industry is a direct result of Ruth's chocolate melting mistake. Nearly one hundred million bags of chocolate chips are sold every year. That's enough to make five billion cookies a year, or fourteen million cookies a day.

the mix, and figured they would melt when the cookies baked. She figured wrong. She stared in amazement at her pan of ruined chocolate-butter drops: cookies speckled with chunks of chocolate. But then, Ruth tasted them. And so did her customers. The result? Undeniably delicious.

As the restaurant grew in popularity, Ruth's Toll House cookies quickly became famous. At the Nestlé candy company, curious sales managers set out to investigate their sudden jump in sales of chocolate bars in the eastern region. They quickly located the source: Ruth Wakefield.

At Ruth's request, Nestlé agreed to score, or cut lines in, their chocolate bars to make them easier to break. Several years later, in 1939, Nestlé decided they could make it easier still. They created the chocolate morsel, or chip, specifically for use in Ruth Wakefield's cookies. They even bought the rights to the Toll House name and, with Ruth's permission, published her recipe right on the back of their chocolate chip package. In exchange, Ruth reportedly was given a lifetime's worth of free chocolate. Today, her invention is still wildly popular. There are countless chocolate chip cookie variations floating around, and new ones pop up regularly. Lots of people are becoming rather creative with their cookies. Some are even adding oats.

Mary Anderson
Windshield Wipers

It was a dreadful day, weatherwise. Snow and sleet pelted the pavement, and people burrowed deep within their coats. Hoping to catch the sights and escape the blustery cold, Mary Anderson of Birmingham, Alabama, climbed aboard a New York City streetcar. The year was 1902. It turned out to be a ride she would never forget, but not because of the scenery. Instead, the ride would inspire her to invent the very first windshield wiper. And simply because she felt sorry for the streetcar driver, who struggled to see through the glass. The invention would not only improve conditions for all drivers, but would save countless lives as well.

Earlier, top-notch engineers had tackled the problem of poor visibility in bad weather and came up with a solution. They split the windshield. Once the glass became covered with rain or snow, the streetcar driver could fling open the mid-

dle for a clear view. Trouble was, it didn't work. At least not very well. Mary watched helplessly as the driver desperately tried to see. When he opened the split glass, he was greeted with a burst of icy cold air and a blast of heavy, wet snow.

"Why doesn't someone create a device to remove the snow?" Mary reportedly asked the people around her.

"It's been tried many times," they told her. *"Can't be done."*

Nonsense, thought Mary, as she scribbled in her notebook. Why can't there be a lever on the inside that would move an arm on the outside to swipe off the

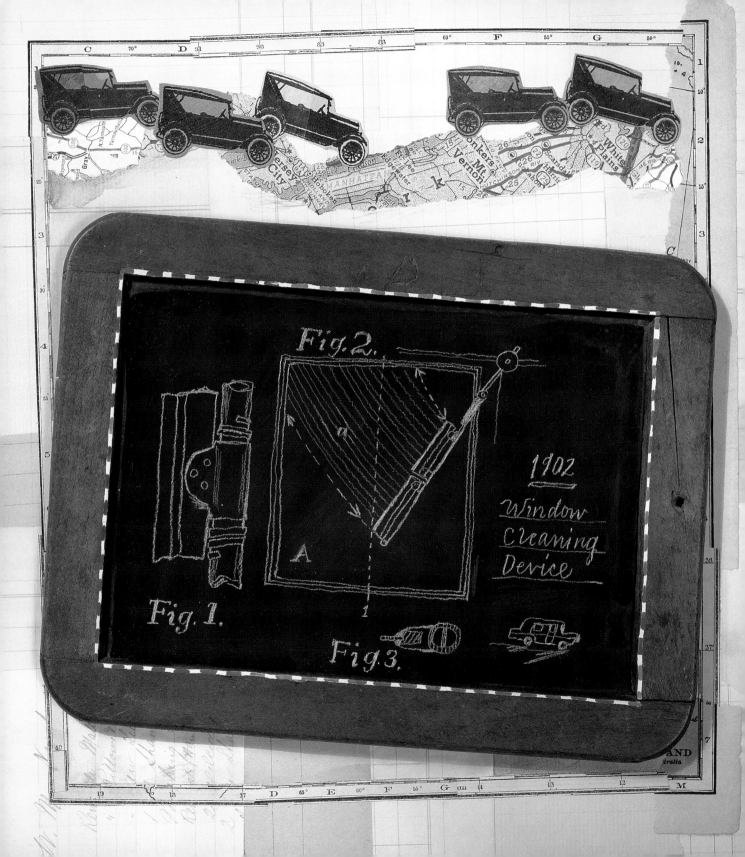

Fig. 2.

1902
Window
Cleaning
Device

Fig. 1.

Fig 3.

A

1

Before windshield wipers were widely available, drivers used to smear pieces of carrots or onions across the glass to create an oily film that they hoped would repel water.

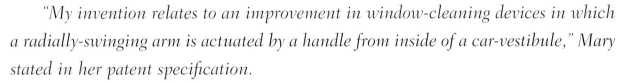

snow? To her, it seemed perfectly simple.

Later, when she returned to her home in Birmingham, she studied her sketches. She spent some time refining her drawings—making them more elaborate, adding more details. Satisfied at last, she brought her design to a small manufacturing company in Birmingham and hired them to make a model. Then, she filed a patent application.

"My invention relates to an improvement in window-cleaning devices in which a radially-swinging arm is actuated by a handle from inside of a car-vestibule," Mary stated in her patent specification.

In other words, a lever on the inside that would move an arm on the outside. Mary's wiper was made of wooden strips and pieces of rubber. She designed it to be removed in good weather so that it would not interfere with the appearance of the streetcar. One of her most important elements was the addition of a counter-weight.

This was used, she writes, "to provide means for maintaining a uniform pressure upon the glass throughout the entire area swept by my improved window-cleaning device."

In other words, it would swipe off the snow. Mary was awarded a patent in 1903 for a window-cleaning device—a windshield wiper. Once the invention was protected by patent, she wrote a large Canadian company offering to sell her rights. They weren't interested. After reviewing her proposal, they decided that her invention had little, if any, commercial value. They simply didn't think it would sell. They encouraged her, however, to submit any other "useful patents" she might have for their consideration.

Mary put the patent in a drawer and, eventually, it expired. Several years later, someone else revived her idea, patented it, sold it, and made a very large sum of money. Every day, lives are saved due to increased visibility during bad weather. Even in our high-tech society, the windshield wiper remains one of the greatest safety inventions of the modern-day automobile. And tourists can now see the sights despite the snow, sleet, or rain.

Stephanie Kwolek
Kevlar®

Skillfully gliding down the snow-packed mountain, a skier is unaware of an amazing material improving the performance of her skis. It is a mysterious material found also in airplanes and athletic shoes. In tires and ropes and gloves. In boats, boots, and bullet-resistant vests.

It's strong—incredibly strong—bullet-stopping strong. It is also flexible and incredibly light—it can shave 800 pounds off an aircraft frame. A material that was once a mere fiction, found only in Superman's suit, is now a fact. Thanks to Stephanie Kwolek, inventor of Kevlar, we now have a fiber that is five times stronger than steel and used in everything from skis and sailboats to space vehicles. As a research chemist for the Du Pont company, Stephanie was assigned to find the next-generation, high-performance fiber.

"At that time, we had heard that there was the potential for a petroleum shortage," explained Stephanie. "We were thinking that if we could get a very strong and very stiff, lightweight fiber, then we could use it to reinforce radial tires. This would make the tires lighter, and therefore you would use less energy because the vehicle would be lighter."

Stephanie spent a few months experimenting with very stiff chain polymers. (A polymer is a chemical compound made up of repeating structural units.) One day she prepared an unusual solution. When she stirred the solution, it turned

ropes
Canoes
Fishing
Rods
Skis
Bullet-
resistant
vests
Boats
Gloves
radial
tires
Airplanes
cables
Sneakers
Golf
Boots

Exposure: 16 hours

% Break Strength Remaining

100
80
60
40
20
0

3 4 5 6 7 10

KEVLAR®

LIGHTER THAN NYLON

STIFFER THAN FIBERGLASS

POLYESTER CAN MELT,
KEVLAR IS NON-MELTING

MORE DURABLE THAN
LEATHER

STRONGER THAN STEEL

MORE THERMAL
STABILITY THAN
ASBESTOS

opalescent—or pearl-like. When she put some on a spatula and let it flow down freely, it was cohesive—like glue. It was also very thin, like water. Amazingly, it was a liquid crystalline solution—part liquid, part solid. Stephanie immediately thought that Du Pont could spin the solution into fiber. But when she took it to a technician, he refused to put it in the spinning apparatus, claiming that the cloudiness and texture of the solution meant there were still bits of solid particles in it—material that would clog the tiny holes of the spinneret.

Kevlar saves lives. Since Du Pont began documenting survivors in 1987, at least 2,274 police officers have been saved by wearing bullet-resistant Kevlar vests. Firefighters are protected with comfortable Kevlar boots that are able to withstand extreme heat and resist sharp objects.

"I went back to the laboratory, and I thought, well, maybe he does have a point," Stephanie said. *"So I filtered it and I found that when the solution passed through a fine-pore glass funnel, it was just as cloudy on the other side, so I knew it didn't have solid material in it."*

Stephanie talked to the technician on and off for a couple of weeks, gently prodding and persuading him to spin her solution. Finally, he agreed. Once the fibers were made, she sent them to the physical-testing lab to have the properties determined—prop-

Once, NASA used a twelve-mile Kevlar cable—thinner than a pencil—to secure a 1,200-pound satellite during a space shuttle mission.

erties like strength and stiffness. The results were astonishing. She had the fibers tested again. And again.

"When I got the numbers back, I was rather skeptical," she recalled. *"I thought maybe they'd made a mistake—and I certainly didn't want to embarrass myself by telling anyone."*

As it turned out, Stephanie didn't embarrass herself. She had invented a remarkable technology and, as a result, a fiber that would forever change the field of polymer chemistry and make many millions of dollars for Du Pont. She was rewarded with a generous bonus and a long-overdue promotion. Many people came on board

As a young girl, Stephanie loved making elaborate paper doll outfits. She would also make outfits from cloth — sneaking in time on her mom's sewing machine. Early on, she had her future career narrowed down to two things: scientist or fashion designer. With the invention of Kevlar, Stephanie got to be both.

during the development phase, and Stephanie is quick to point out that some of them made very significant contributions to the final product. There was a tremendous amount of excitement in the lab — as well as secrecy. And were there any problems?

"There were millions!" said Stephanie, laughing. "Many times we almost gave up because it was such a contrary fiber. And of course before you can commercialize something, the whole process and product have to be very reliable."

Every step was a challenge, she says. Every step a learning process. In 1971, Kevlar fiber was spun in the Du Pont plant for the first time. Today, all you need to do is look around. Kevlar is everywhere. It is used in more than two hundred products, including sailboats, rackets, and racing cars. In downhill skis, woven layers of Kevlar reduce weight and lessen vibration. In athletic shoes, it gives stronger and more flexible foot support and disperses shock. In fact, the product can be used whenever and wherever a very strong, very stiff, lightweight fiber is needed. Any ideas?

Bette Nesmith Graham
Liquid Paper®

It all began with a mistake. Maybe she typed a G instead of an H. Or maybe she left out a word. Regardless, in her determination to solve her typing problems, Bette Nesmith Graham developed a most creative solution. She invented Liquid Paper correction fluid—commonly called "white-out." It was a product that would revolutionize the business world and transform her from an executive secretary at Texas Bank & Trust into a self-made millionaire.

At first, Bette tried to erase her typing errors. But the carbon ribbon used in the new electric typewriter made it impossible. The eraser simply smeared and smudged carbon ink all over her paper. Mistakes were professionally unacceptable, but what could she do?

"I was doing some artwork for Texas Bank on a free-lance basis, trying to make a little extra money," Bette explained. *"And, in lettering, an artist never corrects by erasing, but always paints over the error. So, I decided to use what artists use."*

Bette filled a small glass bottle with tempera water-based paint and, along with a miniature paintbrush, brought it to work. She even colored the paint to blend with the stationery she was using. Her boss never even noticed.

Her coworkers, however, knew she had developed a trick and they continually begged her for her "miracle masking mixture." Finally, five years after she first used her correction fluid, she mixed up a batch of her secret paint to sell to the other secretaries.

"I used a green bottle," Bette recalled. *"I used things I had on hand at home. I*

The Quick Brown fox jumped
over the lazy dog.
The quick brown fox
jumped over The lazy dog.
The quick brown fox jumped
xxxx over the lazy dog.
The quick brown fox jumped oye
over the lazy dog.
The quick brown fox jumped
over the lazy dog.

The quick brownefoxjumped
over the lazy dog!

The quick brown fox jumped over
the lazy dog.

GREGG SHORTHAND

BUSINESS ABBREVIATIONS

F FORMS FOR COMMON W

labor
pretty
even

from,
form
been,
bound
very
before
much

ERASER

Mistake
Out

Dear Madam:

Very truly yours, Yours very truly,

; M I S # 5 T " Ä (K 3 E

9 O 7 U 5 T

History of Correspondence

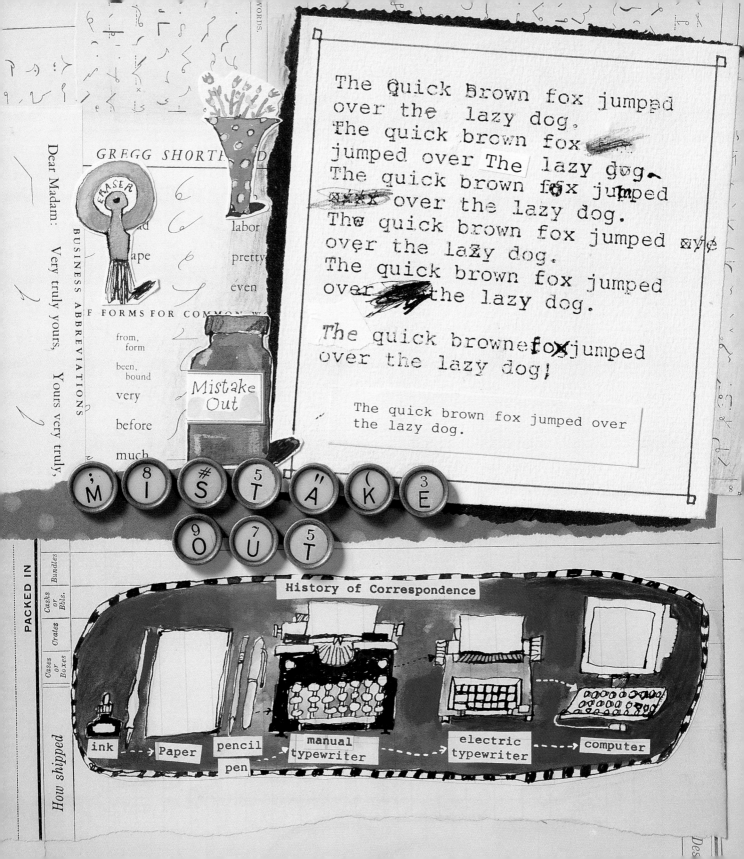

ink ---→ Paper pencil manual typewriter ---→ electric typewriter ---→ computer
pen

Bundles Bunches
Casks or Bbls.
Crates
Cases or Boxes

How shipped

took a file label, wrote 'Mistake Out' on it, and stuck it on the bottle. It was my attempt to be professional."

When she began making batches of Mistake Out, she had a two-room manufacturing plant: her kitchen and her garage. She also had a few employees: her son, Michael, and his friends.

It wasn't long before Bette was supplying all the secretaries at the Texas Bank with her fabulous invention. Several people, including an office supply dealer, strongly encouraged her to market the correction fluid to the general public. However, before she attempted an organized sales campaign, she thought the quality of the paint should be improved. Although it worked, the tempera she had been using took too long to dry and it also left the paper wet. Unfortunately, she couldn't afford to hire a chemist to improve her product.

"I decided I would try to work out a formula myself," she said. "I went to the library and found the formula for a type of tempera paint. A chemistry teacher from St. Mark's School helped me a little bit. I learned how to grind and mix paint from a man at a paint manufacturing company."

Bette changed the name of her correction fluid from Mistake Out to Liquid Paper and set out to market her invention. Less than a year later, a trade publication called *The Office* included a brief article about Liquid Paper in its office supply catalog.

Liquid Paper was first mixed in a five-gallon bucket and then poured into several plastic ketchup bottles. Bette and her employees then filled tiny green jars by squeezing the paint mixture neatly out of the ketchup bottles.

More than five-hundred orders flooded in! The wheels of success had been set in motion. It wasn't long before Bette Nesmith

For several years, Bette signed all her correspondence "B. Nesmith" because, she said, she thought people would take her business more seriously if they believed a man was the president of the company.

Graham had triumphantly conquered the business world with nothing more than a tiny jar, some paint, and a brush. Oh yes, and a lot of ingenuity.

Twenty years after her initial inspiration, Bette sold Liquid Paper to The Gillette Company for $47.5 million dollars. In addition to starting several charitable foundations, she left her son, Michael Nesmith, $25 million. Michael was a popular musician in the 1960s group The Monkees, and he invested much of his inheritance in a production company called Pacific Arts Studio. And, wouldn't you know, Pacific Arts Studio used Michael's investment to become one of the pioneers in the music video industry.

Patsy O. Sherman
Scotchgard™

It's a party: lots of people, lots of laughs, lots of food. Ten unwrapped presents, six spilled sodas, three dropped cupcakes, and two slopped sandwiches later, the party is over. The guests are gone, and the mess is left behind. A stained sofa? A spotted rug? Maybe not.

Spills happen. Sometimes you just wipe up your juice, toss the towel in the sink, and head outside to play soccer. Other times you invent a product that forever changes the textile industry. That's exactly what Patsy O. Sherman did when she invented Scotchgard fabric protector. Hired as a scientist by the 3M laboratories in 1952 on a temporary project, she was supposed to create a new type of fuel hosing to be used on jet aircrafts. One day, while Patsy was making a rubbery synthetic latex mixture, there was an accident.

"A little brown, 4 oz. bottle of this sticky latex mixture was dropped on the floor," Patsy explained. *"It broke—splashed all over the assistant's canvas tennis shoes."*

They tried to clean the white shoes; tried water, tried soap. They used every cleaning solution in the lab, but the spill resisted all attempts. As she noticed the cleaning materials bead up on the splotch, several questions ran through Patsy's mind. Why did this happen? What does it mean? What can be done with it? Eventually, she recognized that her latex mixture could potentially become a fabric treatment that would repel spills and stains—an idea that was unheard of at the time.

Scotchgard	No Scotchgard

29

Scotchgard	No Scotchgard

35

Scotchgard	No Scotchgard

37

Scotchgard	No Scotchgard

48

Scotchgard	No Scotchgard

56

Scotchgard	No Scotchgard

68

Scotchgard	No Scotchgard

106

Scotchgard	No Scotchgard

124

TOMATO SOUP
29

CRAYON
35

COFFEE
37

PAINT
48

INK
56

GRAPE JUICE
68

SODA POP
106

RASPBERRY JAM
124

The actual blob that spilled on the shoe was never ideal for fabric—it was much too sticky, too gummy. Patsy and her co-inventor Sam Smith had to design and create products specifically for use on fabric. Their initial attempts were rather disastrous.

"The first time the product was too sticky. They ran the fabric through the mill and it caused this sticky rubber to build up on the squeeze rolls," recalled Patsy. "The next product we made was a little too hard and too brittle, and when that went through the squeeze rolls it got all hard and powdery."

Patsy received several patents for her fabric protectors, and 3M marketed them under the trademark Scotchgard. Although she didn't receive any money for her inventions, her temporary job became a permanent one—and lasted forty years.

During this experimentation phase, Patsy waited for word of her product's performance. Believe it or not, she couldn't supervise the process because she wasn't even allowed in the textile mills—simply because she was a woman! In the 1950s, discrimination against women was widespread not only in the textile mills, but also in the general workplace. A lot of men assumed that women didn't have the skills or abilities necessary to succeed in business and feared that women would just "get in the way."

"It took a while to get a product to meet the needs of the consumer," says Patsy. "Then we had to learn to prepare it in an economical fashion so the consumer would be willing to pay for it."

After the introduction of Scotchgard in 1956, Patsy spent the next several years improving the product and creating new variations for specific uses and fabrics. She points out that other 3M scientists also became involved in the development of Scotchgard and some of them made very important discoveries.

When the affordable, permanent-press Scotchgard was created, the manager of the manufacturing plant sent a note to 3M stating that they had mixed a large batch of the product and now had a year's supply. A few days later, the entire stock was sold.

But her biggest challenge was yet to come—developing a protector for the new permanent-press fabrics. Because of the nature of the permanent-press fabric, Patsy needed to find something that would both repel stains and release them once the fabric was washed. Impossible, people said. Patsy wasn't so sure. Her first experiments yielded exciting results. The very next day the project had grown so big that every person in the lab was working on it.

"We suddenly had one that everyone wanted to buy," she recalled. *"And that was when the product took off."*

Thanks to an accidental spill and the inventiveness of Patsy Sherman and her colleagues, everyday spills are no longer a problem. Today, there are more than one hundred kinds of Scotchgard protectors and cleaners. The products are sold in more than fifty countries around the world and have made the 3M company millions and millions of dollars. Chances are, most new furniture and carpets are pre-treated with a fabric protector at the factory. So go ahead and spill your soup or slop your pop. Just be sure to clean it up.

Nine years before her invention of Scotchgard, Patsy took a general-interest test in high school. In 1947, girls and boys took separate tests. Despite the fact that she wanted to be a scientist, her test indicated that she was well suited to be a housewife. Unsatisfied, she demanded to take the boy's test. The results? A career in dentistry or chemistry.

Ann Moore
Snugli®

There was always so much to do: work at the computer, work in the yard, go to the store, make lunch, clean up lunch—and all the while keep the baby calm and content. Parents and babysitters everywhere have struggled to hold and comfort their babies while attending to other tasks. What we need, they joked, are more hands. What they got was better.

It began in West Africa with a two-year tour of duty in the Peace Corps. As a pediatric nurse, Ann Moore had plenty of opportunities to observe babies, their mothers, and the closeness they shared. The African babies were always cradled in bright cloth wraps and slung on their mothers' backs, and Ann noticed that they seemed very secure and content. Back home, with the birth of her own baby, Ann was determined to recreate the comfort and convenience of the African carrier. And that's exactly what she did. Along the way, her creation just happened to spark a multimillion-dollar business: the Snugli baby pouch.

"I tried the African method," Ann explained. *"It's just a piece of fabric about three yards long. They balance the baby on their back and then tie this long piece of fabric around their chest and waist. I could never make that stay," said Ann, laughing. "After a little while, the baby would always slide down my back and I felt very insecure with that."*

So Ann turned to her mother, Lucy Aukerman, for help. Using photos from the African trip as a model, Ann's mom fashioned a cloth baby carrier that was more functional and easier to wear. The carrier was a cozy pouch with two holes

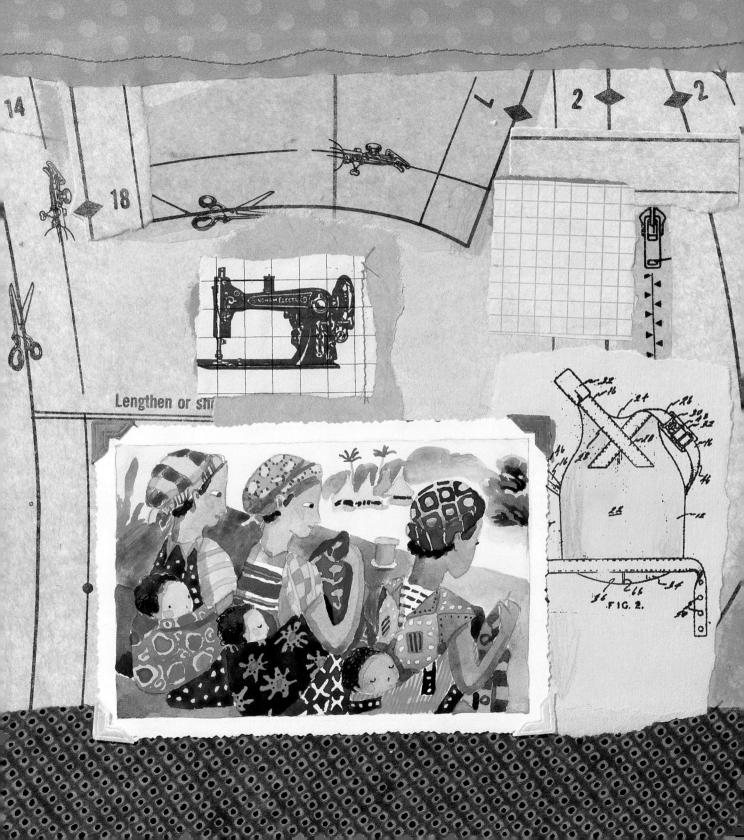

for the baby's legs and shoulder straps to fasten it to Ann's back.

"We had no thought of ever marketing it," recalled Ann. "It was just for me to have my hands free and have a happy baby."

It worked wonderfully. Everywhere Ann went, people commented on her ingenious baby carrier. "Where can I get one?" they would ask.

"So my mother would make one for them, and I'd send it off," explained Ann. "That's how it all started and how it grew really—just by word of mouth."

It was 1965, and Ann and her mother were selling two baby carriers a month. When their carrier was mentioned in the *Whole Earth Catalogue*, sales instantly jumped to eighteen a month. Now it was time to get serious. Ann, her mother, and her husband, Mike, brainstormed for a name. Mike quit his job to work on marketing the Snugli full-time. They applied for a patent and formed a company. They designed special packaging and made minor improvements.

The packaging of Snuglis was done in a long, cinder-block building—a converted dog kennel. And the handmade versions were created in a production facility on Ann's parents' farm—in a converted chicken house.

"The first one did not have adjustable shoulder straps," said Ann. "I hadn't realized that I had to get it over coats and thicker things. So then we had to figure out a way to make it adjustable."

The demand for Snuglis continued to grow. By the early 1970s, Ann's company was hand-making and selling three hundred carriers a month. And then . . .

"In 1975, Consumer Reports *did a little review of baby carriers and they said the Snugli was the best," explained Ann.*

Over the years, Ann has received several photos from zookeepers carrying baby animals. It seems that some zoo animals — including baby chimps and baby kangaroos — find the Snugli cozy and comfortable too.

Then the company really took off. By 1979, they had designed a new version of the Snugli—with a stiffer fabric that could be reproduced in a factory. They still sold the handmade versions, but the factory-made ones offered customers a less costly alternative. Now the Snugli company was making *eight thousand* carriers by hand and twenty-five thousand in the factory every month. By 1984, yearly sales had reached $6 million. After several different offers, Ann and Mike finally sold the company in 1985 to the Huffy Corporation. And for moms and pops and babies on the go, Ann Moore's Snugli has become a necessity, a must-have, a what-in-the-world-would-we-do-without-it sort of product. In short, who needs more hands?

Grace Murray Hopper
Computer Compiler

No one thought it was possible. Giving a computer commands in English—using words rather than mathematical code—was said to be a ridiculous idea. And creating a method that allowed for automatic programming was also considered laughable. But for mathematician and navy officer Grace Murray Hopper, such ideas were not only logical, they were also necessary and inevitable. When Grace created the first computer compilers, she paved the way for computer programming as we know it today. The high-level computer languages that run our banks, our businesses, and our government have been developed by drawing upon her innovations. Even computer games descend from her pioneer work in programming. For the first time, Grace's compilers allowed nonmathematicians to use computers for many different tasks both in business and for private use.

"No one thought of that earlier because they weren't as lazy as I was," Grace said. "A lot of our programmers liked to play with the bits. I wanted to get jobs done. That's what the computer was there for."

In the beginning, when computers were first being developed, Grace and her fellow mathematicians did the programming by using mathematical code—plugging in numbers as commands. A combination of zeros and ones would have a specific meaning. For example, if Grace wanted to stop the computer, she would enter "1001100." She had to enter every program individually—even when many of them shared several of the same steps. This method was not only very time-

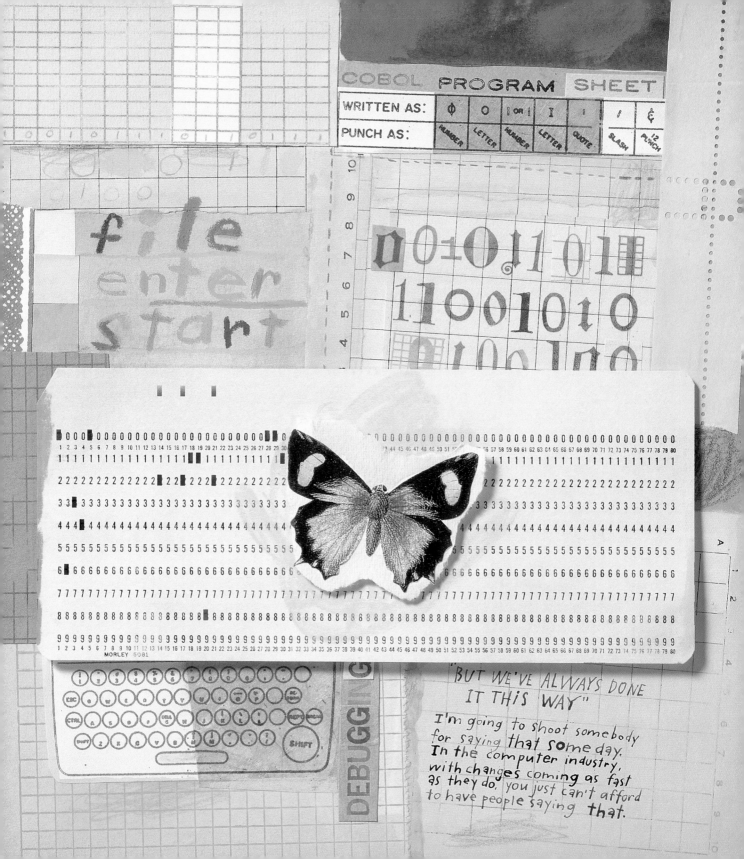

COBOL PROGRAM SHEET

WRITTEN AS:	Ø	O	1 OR I	1	'	/	&
PUNCH AS:	NUMBER	LETTER	NUMBER	LETTER	QUOTE	SLASH	12 PUNCH

file
enter
start

10 01011010
11001010
010010

MORLEY 5081

DEBUGGING

"BUT WE'VE ALWAYS DONE
IT THIS WAY"

I'm going to shoot somebody
for saying that some day.
In the computer industry,
with changes coming as fast
as they do, you just can't afford
to have people saying that.

consuming but, as Grace pointed out, it was also extremely easy to make mistakes. One incorrect number could ruin the whole program.

"It was so obvious," stated Grace. *"Why start from scratch with every single program you write? Develop one that would do a lot of the basic work over and over again. Developing a compiler was a logical move."*

Logical, that was, for Grace. For her colleagues and superiors at the Remington Rand company, a computer compiler was considered undoable.

Grace proved otherwise. In 1952, she developed the A-0 System—a program, or set of instructions, that could transform

Grace kept a clock in her office that ran counterclockwise — or backward. It was a daily reminder to herself and anyone who visited her office that things could, in fact, be done differently. According to Grace, the worst phrase in the English language is "But we've always done it that way."

mathematical code into machine code. To do this, she plucked specific pieces of code from several programs and gave each piece an individual call number so she could locate it and arrange it in the order needed. She then combined the separate pieces of code onto magnetic tape.

"All I had to do was to write down a set of call numbers, let the computer find them on the tape, bring them over, and do the additions," explained Grace. *"This was the first compiler. We could start writing mathematical equations and let the computer do the work."*

With the success of her A-0 compiler, she moved ahead to develop the B-0 System, a compiler that could understand instructions given in English (later to be called FLOWMATIC). Her new compiler, she explained, would act as a translator of sorts—converting letters of the alphabet into the recognizable language of machine code. Her goal? To create a user-friendly computer. Once again, Grace was told, "It can't be done." But once again, she did it anyway.

"When you have a good idea and you've tried it and you know it's going to work, go ahead and do it," she said, *"because it is much easier to apologize later than it is to get permission."*

By 1957, Grace's FLOWMATIC was one of three computer programming languages used in American computers, and the only one that could understand English commands. It quickly became apparent, however, that a universal computer language was necessary—one language that could be used to run all computers. And Grace's position? Leading the movement for standardization. Without a single language, she insisted, the entire computer industry would be "dead in the water."

Grace Hopper's innovative compilers ultimately served as road maps for the development of COBOL (COmmon Business Oriented Language), the first universal computer language to be used in government and business computers. And thanks to her user-friendly programming ideas, today's high-level programming languages were made possible. High-level languages, for example, that drive computer games. Now all you have to do is figure out how to win them.

In the summer of 1945, Grace and her colleagues were working on the enormous, fifty-foot-long IBM computer called the Mark II when suddenly the computer stopped. Upon investigation, they discovered that a moth had gotten in and caused a relay to fail. They carefully removed the moth and taped it in their logbook along with the notation "first actual case of a bug being found." From then on, when their supervisor asked why they weren't calculating faster, they told him they were busy "debugging" the computer. The term has been with us ever since.

Margaret E. Knight
Paper Bags

They're used every minute of every hour of every day by millions of people in thousands of stores across the United States and throughout the world. When she invented a machine that made flat-bottomed paper bags, Margaret E. Knight not only revolutionized the paper bag industry, but she forever changed the way people shopped. No longer did they have to pack their milk, meats, and cheeses into heavy, wooden crates. No longer did shoppers struggle to stuff jam and bread into bags shaped like envelopes. With the flat-bottomed paper bag, life suddenly got a whole lot easier.

Margaret's job at the Columbia Paper Bag Company was relatively simple. She needed to gather, stack, and tie the company's finished bags into neat bundles. Regular bags were made by machine; flat-bottomed bags by hand. She had been at work barely a week before the idea came to her.

"I had plenty of leisure time for making observations," Margaret said. "And such time was employed in watching the movement of the machines and the manufacture of square-bottomed bags by hand."

Why did flat-bottomed bags have to be made by hand, she wondered? It was time-consuming and very costly. Few customers could afford them. Margaret was told there was no such thing as a machine that could fold and paste flat bottoms. This seemed odd to her since the flat bottom was clearly a better bag.

Margaret had no formal training in engineering, but she had been working with or around machines—in cotton mills and manufacturing plants—from her earliest memory. In fact, as a child, she much preferred a jackknife, gimlet, and

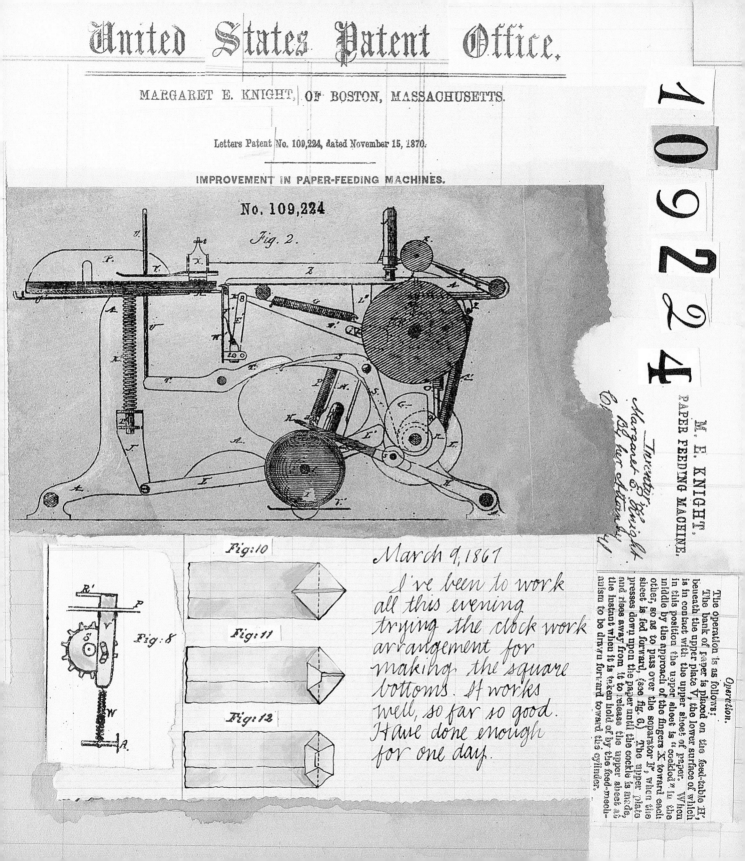

United States Patent Office.

MARGARET E. KNIGHT, OF BOSTON, MASSACHUSETTS.

Letters Patent No. 109,224, dated November 15, 1870.

IMPROVEMENT IN PAPER-FEEDING MACHINES.

No. 109,224

Fig. 2.

Fig: 8

Fig: 10

Fig: 11

Fig: 12

March 9, 1867

I've been to work all this evening trying the clock work arrangement for making the square bottoms. It works well, so far so good. Have done enough for one day.

10 9 2 2 4

M. E. KNIGHT.
PAPER FEEDING MACHINE.

Twenty-Eight
Margaret E. Knight
By her Attorney

Operation.

The operation is as follows:

The bank of paper is placed on the feed-table H', beneath the upper plate V; the lower surface of which is in contact with the upper sheet of paper. When in this position the upper sheet is "cockled" in the middle by the approach of the fingers X toward each other, so as to pass over the separator P', when the sheet is fed forward, (see fig. 6.) The upper plate presses down upon the paper until the cockle is made, and rises away from it to release the upper sheet at the instant when it is taken hold of by the feed-mechanism to be drawn forward toward the cylinder.

pieces of wood to dolls and other such toys.

She began by making drawings of her ideas. Next, she constructed a cutting tool that she called a guide finger, and created a folding tool from a piece of tin that she called a plate-knife folder. The result? A successfully folded square-bottomed bag.

"Been to work all this evening trying the clockwork arrangement for making the square bottoms," Margaret writes in her diary on Saturday, March 9, 1867. "It works well, so far so good. Have had enough for one day. If other parts work as well I shall be satisfied."

"My next experiment was on one of my machines in the shop, to which I rigged these same two devices, my guide finger and plate-knife folder," she explained. "By this means the paper tube followed along the guide finger entering it and flushing it back over the plate-knife folder. I did succeed in folding square bottoms."

Once she established that a machine could, in fact, fold and paste square bottoms, Margaret was more determined then ever. A year after her initial idea, she successfully built a wooden model, about two and a half feet in length and one foot wide.

"In July of 1868, I then completed making it a perfect working model," stated Margaret. "I should say that I made thousands of bags from it."

She then hired a skilled machinist to build an iron version, which she needed to submit along with her patent application. Unfortunately, and unknown to Margaret, a man named Charles Annan saw her machine in the shop while it was being cast in iron. He copied it and tried to patent it as his own.

Determined to set the record straight, Margaret went to Washington, D.C., with her diary, patterns, photos, records, models, folded bags, witnesses, and her lawyer in tow to fight Annan's claims before the commissioner of patents.

After sixteen days of testimony, she won. The invention of the machine that makes flat-bottomed paper bags was acknowledged as Margaret Knight's and she was awarded a patent in 1870. She joined forces with a business partner and established the Eastern Paper Bag Company in Hartford, Connecticut, to manufacture her machines. She also set up a lab where she worked on other inventions—amassing a total of twenty-seven patents—and prompting the media of the time to dub her "Lady Edison."

Although Margaret's invention has stood the test of time, she didn't get rich. Reportedly, she was offered $50,000 for her machine — the equivalent of more than half a million dollars today — but turned it down. It was noteworthy, then, that at her death her estate was worth a mere $275.05.

Margaret Knight's paper bag machine remains a milestone in the history of mechanical engineering. It's remarkable that during this era of high-tech gadgetry, a simple paper bag has remained a staple of everyday life. So, shoppers, toss some more chips and salsa into your cart. Your bag will hold them.

Jeanne Lee Crews
Space Bumper

Jeanne plopped a chunk of metal—deformed by a deep crater—on her manager's desk. "We absolutely must do something!" she declared. She was referring to the problem of orbital debris in space—stuff like rocks, sand, and bits of metal that can crash into a satellite, shuttle, or space station. She had the prop to prove the devastating affects of a collision: destroyed space vehicles, destroyed experiments, destroyed lives.

"It's unbelievable the damage that can be done by things going at that speed," explains Jeanne. *"I really cared about this problem—it was a safety thing—so I persisted and became a real pain."*

Finally, Jeanne Lee Crews, an aerospace engineer at NASA's Johnson Space Center, was given the green light to tackle the problem. Her goal was to find a lightweight shield that could withstand the extreme elements of space and protect the craft from debris—a space bumper of sorts. Her ingenuity sparked the development of several space shields— inventions that the space program could no longer safely function without.

Space debris travels at a speed of eighteen thousand miles per hour. That's three hundred miles per minute, and five miles per second. If you could travel at that speed, you could get to a store two and a half miles away—and back home—in one second.

The first part of the problem—coming up with the concept—was the easy part. Instead of using one thick shield of aluminum, the most commonly used shield, Jeanne would create a space bumper made of multiple layers. The next step was her toughest challenge: determining what materials to use and how to

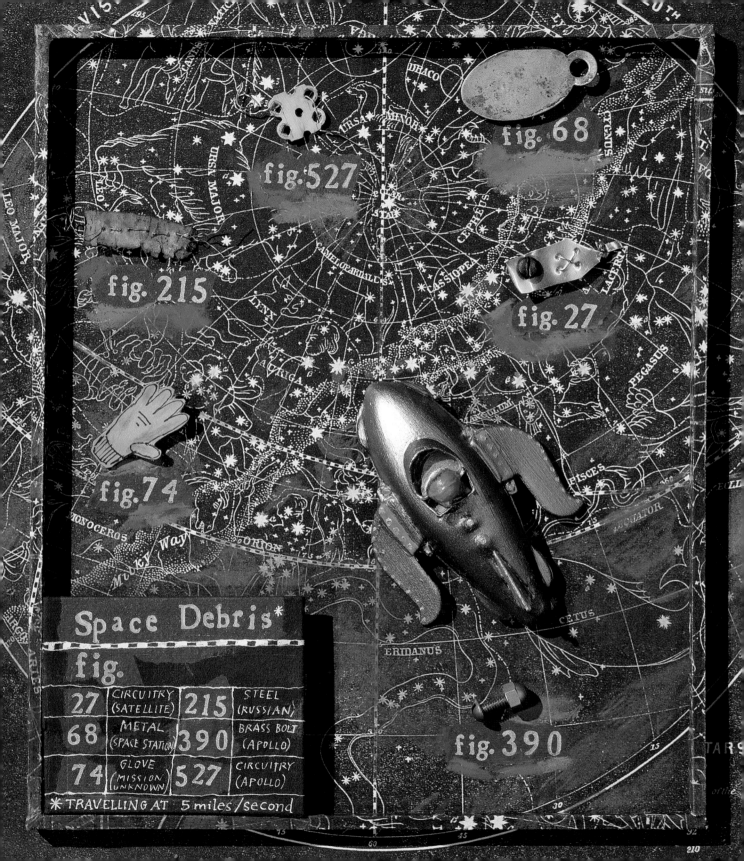

fig. 68

fig. 527

fig. 215

fig. 27

fig. 74

fig. 390

Space Debris*
fig.

27	CIRCUITRY (SATELLITE)	215	STEEL (RUSSIAN)
68	METAL (SPACE STATION)	390	BRASS BOLT (APOLLO)
74	GLOVE (MISSION UNKNOWN)	527	CIRCUITRY (APOLLO)

* TRAVELLING AT 5 miles/second

assemble them effectively. Jeanne came up with a creative solution: a ceramic fabric commonly used to line furnaces.

"We took this Nextel™ ceramic fabric and put it in a bunch of thin layers and created a flexible shield that had a really powerful shocker effect," Jeanne explained. *"It shocks a particle once and then again and again and again."*

Shocking a particle (creating shock waves on impact) causes it to become fragmented, or break apart. After designing and constructing the shield, Jeanne tested it for performance and workability. Of course she couldn't test it in space, but there was another option. In a 150-foot-long, metal building, Jeanne's team experimented. They simulated the conditions of a crash in space by using a high-tech tool called a light-gas gun.

"The biggest gun is about a hundred feet long, and we have a very high speed camera that goes a million frames per second," Jeanne said. *"We take x-rays of the bullet while it's in flight. The guns are actually very simple. It's the diagnostics— making it all work together—that is the difficult part."*

Months later, Jeanne successfully created the multishock shield, a combination of four layers of the ceramic fabric with three inches of air space in between. The total weight? Less than one sheet of aluminum. But now she had a new problem: designing a shield for the crew modules—the astronauts' living quarters—on the International Space Station. The modules had only four and a half inches of room for a shield, so the foot-thick multishock couldn't be used. Ever inventive, Jeanne and her coworkers simply modified the multishock shield— compressing it, or flattening it, and adding a new material. Maybe you've heard of it? . . . Kevlar.

Jeanne explained how the shield works. "First there's a piece of aluminum out-

side the spacecraft that breaks up the debris. A particle busts through that, gets broken up some, and hits the Nextel™ ceramic and then gets broken up a whole bunch."

Now, she said, there are still moving pieces that have tremendous energy—but they are slowed down considerably; to about the speed of a bullet, or one kilometer per second.

"So the Kevlar's behind the ceramic fabric and it slows it down again—so nothing gets to the back sheet," she said. "And that's the shield we're using on the space station."

The shields invented by Jeanne Crews and her coworkers are patented and belong to their employer, NASA. They are shields that will protect the astronauts, the space station, and critical experiments—experiments that are best carried out in the ideal conditions offered in space: particularly that of microgravity (which is as close to zero gravity as we can come). Already, as a result of the knowledge gained through experimentation and exploration in space, we are able to enjoy hundreds of exciting products and reap the benefits of significant scientific advancements, including heart-rate monitors, diabetic pumps, bike helmets, and satellite TV. And who knows what else might be discovered in space? Maybe a nifty high-tech tennis racket, or just maybe, a promising cure for cancer.

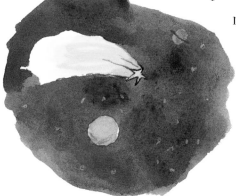

Valerie L. Thomas
Illusion Transmitter

Welcome to the future—where technology promises exciting adventures. Like the illusion transmitter. When mathematician Valerie L. Thomas invented a device for displaying the three-dimensional illusion of an object—without using a laser—she took what once belonged only to scientists and science-fiction writers and created a tool for the average person. With Valerie's invention, actors would move about—as if in real life—in the viewer's own living room, or family room, or kitchen.

"You know those 3-D glasses where it seems like the picture is coming out of the frame?" Valerie asked, as she explained how her transmitter worked. "You have a similar effect, but you don't have to put on special glasses. Assume that you have a TV set without a screen on it, and you have an open area instead. The image comes out of this open area and displays in front of it in the air."

Curiosity led to her creation. As the manager of development of image processing for NASA's Goddard Space Center, Valerie had a natural interest in attending science fairs. Once, while observing a demonstration at one of these fairs, a lightbulb caught her eye. From a distance, she watched as the demonstrator unscrewed the bulb and took it out. All perfectly normal, except that the lightbulb appeared to stay in the lamp—and more than that, it looked as though it was still on. What was happening? wondered Valerie as she went over to investigate. Intrigued, she reached out to touch the bulb, but her hand sailed smoothly through it. She decided right then and there that she would find out

PROCESSOR   TRANSCEIVER

how it worked.

After researching real images in optics, or the study of light, Valerie had a better understanding of what was happening.

"Once I understood the concept," she explained, "I started thinking about how it could be used for practical applications. Which is when I thought about a TV-type of application, which could transmit images and have them appear in the air in your house rather than on a screen."

So with the help of her able assistant, Mark, Valerie experimented in her lab—a lab that doubled as her living room and dining room. Mark was as enthusiastic and as curious as she was. He was also her five-year-old son. Valerie used things around the house, improvising when she didn't have exactly what she needed. No concave mirror? A spoon would work fine, she thought. And maybe some masking tape and a Christmas candle. After some initial success, she went out and got several mirrors for serious testing. Testing her discovery was not without problems and frustrations.

A three-dimensional image is known as a "real image." It is formed with a rounded, concave mirror and appears to have depth — like a real object. The image is produced in the space in front of the mirror. Take a look at the inside curve of a shiny spoon. What do you see?

"Once when I was experimenting with a new mirror," Valerie said, "I was having some difficulty finding where in space the image was being projected. And I was thinking, It doesn't seem to be working. Maybe my idea will not work! And then I heard, 'Mommy, Mommy! Here it is, right here!' So then I got excited again."

Although she patented the illusion transmitter in 1980, she doesn't have an available product. Yet. Her main problem, said Valerie, was being able to take the idea to the next level—finding the necessary resources to make a working model and manufacture actual units. Also, transmitting television shows in 3-D would require the cooperation of network programmers, a potentially large obstacle. But, she said, even without the networks you would be able to transmit your own images, like your home videos.

The illusion transmitter has a receiver that looks like a TV but has no screen. It has a concave mirror on the transmitting end, and another one on the receiving end to recreate the real image once it's been received. It then picks up and processes signals in much the same way that a television does.

So what will the future hold? Already, others have developed similar products, which are slowly being introduced to the market. And so Valerie Thomas has a hunch that an invention made from mirrors might one day be as common as computers or TV sets. An invention that brings your favorite actor—or maybe an African elephant or the space shuttle—right into your living room. It may only be an illusion, but it sure is cool.

Girls (Even the Young Ones) Think of Everything

Becky Schroeder

A person has to be sixteen to drive, seventeen to see certain movies, and eighteen to vote. People can get terrific discounts on all sorts of stuff—provided they're over sixty-five. Everywhere we look there are age limits that define what people can and can't do. But creativity has no boundaries, no limitations. Anyone can invent. And they do. Inventors are popping up at the youngest of ages.

Sitting in the car waiting for her mom to return from shopping, Becky decided she might as well try to finish her math homework. But it was growing dark and getting hard to see the paper.

"I didn't have a flashlight, and I didn't want to open the car door because then the whole car would light up," recalled Becky. "So I thought it would be neat to have my paper light up somehow, and that's when the idea came to me."

It isn't every day that a ten-year-old invents a product eagerly sought by several businesses, but that's exactly what Becky Schroeder did when she created a tool that enabled people to write in the dark. Her invention? The Glo-sheet.

That night Becky went home trying to imagine different ways of making her paper glow in the dark. She remembered all sorts of glow-in-the-dark toys—like balls and Frisbees™—and wondered how they were

After reading about Becky's invention, NASA sent her a letter. They wanted to know if she was a former employee because the Glo-sheet sounded similar to one of their projects (and if so, they would own her patent). They had no idea she was a kid.

47

Attorney Docket Number	
First Named Inventor	Becky Schroeder

UTILITY OR

COMPLETE IF KNOWN

Things that glow in the dark:

man made

flashlights
candles
Frisbee™

Sticker stars
(that you put on
your ceiling).

the moon

in nature

fireflies
phosphorescent
fish:

stars and planets
glow-worms

It worked! The paper glowed. I painted stacks of paper in the bathroom, (and other parts of the house)

As a below named inventor, I hereby declare that:

I believe I am the original, first and sole inventor (if only one name is listed below) or an original, first and joint inventor (if plural names are listed below) of the subject matter which is claimed and for which a patent is sought on the invention entitled:

GLO SHEET

the specification of which
☐ is attached hereto
OR
☐ was filed on (MM/DD/YYYY)

(Title of the Invention)

Application Number _____ as United States Application Number or PCT International

I hereby state that _____ (YYYY) _____
amended by

made. She was determined to find a solution. So the very next day, Becky's dad took her on an outing to the hardware store. They returned with a pail of phosphorescent paint. She took the paint and stacks of paper into the darkest room in the house—the bathroom. There, she experimented.

"I'd turn on the light, turn it off, turn it on," said Becky. "My parents remember me running out of the room saying, 'It works, it works! I'm writing in the dark!'"

She used an acrylic board and coated it with a specific amount of phosphorescent paint. She took a complicated idea and made it work rather simply. When the coated clipboard is exposed to light, it glows. The glowing board then illuminates, or lights up, the paper that has been placed on top. Two years after her initial inspiration, in 1974, Becky became the youngest female ever to receive a U.S. patent.

She didn't actively market her Glo-sheet. She didn't need to. The *New York Times* wrote an article about an incredible invention—patented by a twelve-year-old—and the inquiries and orders streamed in. Professionals who needed to

write in the dark started ordering her Glo-sheet: photographers for their darkrooms, critics who took notes in darkened theaters, emergency medical people for use in ambulances.

"Some of the Glo-sheets I was handmaking and some I had a company manufacture for me," Becky explained. "There were more expensive versions and less expensive ones—electric-operated and light-activated models."

Several large companies offered to buy her patent rights, but Becky and her father decided to sell the Glo-sheet on their own. What began as a personal project, just for fun, blossomed into a business, with Becky as the president of the company. Proof that success can come at any age with a good idea and a little imagination.

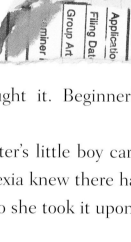

Alexia Abernathy

And here's more proof. One day, about a dozen managers at some very large companies received a letter in the mail. "Hi. I'm Alexia Abernathy, and I'm an eleven-year-old inventor." Based on that letter, six companies asked for more information on her product—the no-spill feeding bowl. One company eventually bought it. Beginner's luck? Maybe. A great idea? Definitely.

Every morning, it was the same story. Her babysitter's little boy carried his breakfast to the table, spilling every step of the way. Alexia knew there had to be a way to stop the cereal from slopping over the sides. So she took it upon herself to do something about it.

"The idea actually came pretty easily," said Alexia. "I was just thinking, OK, he's walking and spilling over the side, so what you need is some way to collect what spills. And I thought, what if you had a bigger bowl to hold onto it?"

At the time, she was involved in the program "Invent, Iowa!" through her elementary school and had to come up with an invention anyway and thought this would be a good, practical problem to solve. So Alexia created the nonslosh bowl—a product that, within a couple of years, would find its way onto the shelves of major stores like Toys 'R' Us, Wal-Mart, and Target.

Alexia Abernathy

rim

handles

cereal or soup

Big bowl

small bowl

Inventor's signature(s):

Alexia Abernathy

DATE: January 17, 1992

My dad suggested a new problem, that was Charlie, (our babysitters 2½ year old). So I began to think of things he does and things he gets into. That's when it hit me, just this morning when he was walking to the table he spilled half his milk and cereal out of the bowl onto the floor. So my new invention is, that you have a little bowl super glued

FIG. 2

Little Kids

Oops!Proof™

NO-SPILL FEEDING BOWL

Prevents messy meal spills!
Bowl-within-a-bowl catches spills before they happen!

"I thought I needed the simplest materials possible," she explained. "So I went and bought Tupperware™ bowls. My dad helped me cut the top out of one of the containers to form a rim. And the only thing I had to do was put the small bowl inside the large bowl."

When the Little Kids company bought Alexia's invention in 1994, they changed the name to Oops! Proof No-Spill Feeding Bowl and made the bowls so they could snap together. They also added a piece that makes it completely spillproof.

Originally, Alexia wanted the bowls to snap together but didn't have the materials or means to do that, so she settled for glue. She experimented with all sorts of glues, but nothing worked. The bowls always came apart when they were being washed. Eventually, she tried hot glue, and finally it held. That was it; she was done. She entered her clear, nonslosh bowl with the blue lid in the "Invent, Iowa!" contest and won. She advanced to the next two levels of the contest, but ultimately lost at the state competition. Encouraged by others who saw her invention, Alexia decided to try and market her bowl. So she wrote her letters.

"If everyone would have said no, I never would have pursued it," confessed Alexia. "It wasn't like I was doing this for money; it was just kind of fun."

But she did get money. She got her name on a patent, and she got to see her invention sitting on the shelves of major stores. Just think what else could be done with a simple idea, a solid solution, and a stack of first-class stamps. And it really *doesn't* matter how old you are. . . .

Your Turn

Suppose you have an invention of your own. It's different, it's new, it's neat. Now what? Obtaining a patent may be an important first step. A patent is the legal document issued by the government to protect an idea. Utility patents are for inventions that are either mechanical or electrical in nature. Design patents cover inventions that are new and original designs of existing products.

To patent an invention, you must prove that it is new and useful and that you are the very first person to have invented the item. It is important that you apply for a patent immediately, and you are required to use a patent attorney or patent agent to do so. A patent application must be complete with diagrams, notes, and models. If your invention proves to be unique, you pay the fees and are assigned a patent number. Your invention is then legally protected for twenty years (from the date of filing), and you alone have the right to profit from it.

Not all inventions, however, will benefit from having a patent. The patent process can be extremely expensive, and depending on the invention, might not be really necessary. A good patent attorney should be able to advise you on the merits of obtaining a patent for your specific invention.

For more information on the patent process, contact:

U.S. Patent and Trademark Office
Washington, D.C. 20231
(800) 786-9199
www.uspto.gov

There are several contests and organizations that encourage young people to use their creativity. The following is a small sample of what's available. Check your local library for additional listings.

Camp Invention
National Invention Center
221 South Broadway
Akron, Ohio 44308
(800) 968-IDEA
www.invent.org

Duracell/NSTA Scholarship Competition
National Science Teachers Association
1840 Wilson Boulevard
Arlington, Virginia 22201
(703) 243-7100
www.NSTA.org

Inventors Clubs of America
P.O. Box 450261
Atlanta, Georgia 31145-0261
(770) 938-5089

Young Inventors and Creators Program
National Inventive Thinking Association
P.O. Box 836202
Richardson, Texas 75083
or
Office of Public Affairs
U.S. Patent and Trademark Office
Washington, D.C. 20231
(703) 305-8341

Further Reading

Karnes, Frances A., Ph.D., and Suzanne M. Bean, Ph.D. *Girls and Young Women Inventing.* Minneapolis: Free Spirit Publishing, 1995.

Lee, J.A.N. "Unforgettable Grace Hopper," *Reader's Digest,* October 1994, pp. 181–85.

McKeown, Blanche. "She Invented the Windshield Wiper," *The Record,* January 1956, pp. 10–12.

Macdonald, Anne L. *Feminine Ingenuity: Women and Invention in America.* New York: Ballantine, 1992.

Reeves, Lynn. "Concern Gave Boon to Drivers," *Birmingham News,* February 13, 1972, pp. 10–12.

Showell, Ellen H., and Fred M. B. Amram. *From Indian Corn to Outer Space: Women Invent in America.* Peterborough, N. H.: Cobblestone Publishing, 1995.

Stallworth, Clarke. "Southern Belle Invented Wiper for Windshield," *Birmingham News,* February 20, 1977.

Stanley, Autumn. *Mothers and Daughters of Invention: Notes for a Revised History of Technology.* Metuchen, N. J.: Scarecrow Press, 1993.

Vare, Ethlie Ann, and Greg Ptacek. *Mothers of Invention: From the Bra to the Bomb, Forgotten Women and their Unforgettable Ideas.* New York: William Morrow, 1988.

———. *Women Inventors and their Discoveries.* Minneapolis: Oliver Press, 1993.

Sources

Abernathy, Alexia. Interview by author. Tape recording (telephone). Minneapolis, April 17, 1998.

Billings, Charlene W. *Grace Hopper: Navy Admiral and Computer Pioneer.* Hillside, N.J.: Enslow, 1989.

Crews, Jeanne Lee. Interview by author. Tape recording (telephone). Minneapolis, February 10, 1998.

Kwolek, Stephanie. Interview by author. Tape recording (telephone). Minneapolis, January 20, 1998.

"Liquid Paper Corporation History" in "Letter Perfect" employee newsletter. Boston: The Gillette Company, April 1980.

Moore, Ann. Interview by author. Tape recording (telephone). Minneapolis, June 17, 1998.

Perry, Rebecca Schroeder. Interview by author. Tape recording (telephone). Minneapolis, February 10, 1998.

Sherman, Patsy O. Interview by author. Tape recording. Bloomington, Minnesota, January 13, 1998.

Thomas, Valerie L. Interview by author. Tape recording (telephone). Minneapolis, March 13, 1998.

U.S. Patent and Trademark Office: Before the Commissioner of Patents. "Testimony for Margaret E. Knight; Deposition of Margaret E. Knight." Boston, May 5, 1870.

U.S. Patent Office. "Specification forming part of Letters Patent No. 743,801," Mary Anderson, of Birmingham, Alabama, Window-Cleaning Device. November 10, 1903.

Acknowledgments

The author wishes to thank the following for their contributions:

Du Pont; Katherine Hagmeier, 3M; Roz O'Hearn, Nestlé; Ellen Walley, NASA; Carrie Ahlborn, Brewster Academy; Eunice McSweeney, Whitman Historical Commission; U. S. Patent and Trademark Office; Danielle Frizi, The Gillette Company; Stanley Bauman Photography; Herral Long Photography; Dr. Roger F. Murray II; A'Lelia Bundles/Madam Walker Family Collection; Charlene Billings; J.A.N. Lee; Ann Moore; Alexia Abernathy; Patsy Sherman; Stephanie Kwolek; Jeanne Crews; Rebecca Schroeder Perry; Valerie L. Thomas.

Index

1946	**Dorothy Rodgers** *Jonny Mop*
1947	**Alice King Chatham** *helmet used by Chuck Yeager when he broke the sound barrier*
1948	**Rachel Brown and Elizabeth Hazen** *Nystatin (antibiotic drug)*
1950ʌ	**Anna Kalso** *earth shoes*
1950ʌ	**Rosalyn Yalow** *radioimmunoassay (medical tool)*
1951	**Marion Donovan** *disposable diaper*
1952	**Grace Murray Hopper** *computer compiler*
1952	**Virginia Apgar** *Apgar Score*
1953	**Gertrude Elion** *wonder drugs for treatment of leukemia and kidney transplant rejection*
1956	**Patsy O. Sherman** *Scotchgard*
1957	**Bette Nesmith Graham** *Liquid Paper*
1959	**Ruth Handler** *Barbie Doll™*
1960	**Teresa and Mary Thompson (eight and nine years old)** *solar teepee*
1965	**Ann Moore** *Snugli baby carrier*
1966	**Mary Davidson Kenner** *carrier attachment for walking aide*
1968	**Betty Galloway (ten years old)** *bubble-making toy*
1969	**Pansy Ellen Essman** *Pansey-ette bath aid (sponge pillow to keep babies secure in the bath)*
1971	**Stephanie Kwolek** *Kevlar*
1971	**Erna Schneider Hoover** *telephone switching system*
1974	**Becky Schroeder** *Glo-sheet*
1975	**Barbara Askins** *Autoradiograph (photographic technique for NASA)*
1975	**Virgie M. Ammons** *fireplace damper actuating tool*
1975	**Ruth Siems** *instant stuffing mix*
1980ʌ	**Cheryl Moore** *pressure-sensitive adhesives*
1980ʌ	**Connie Hubbard (& Ray Heyer)** *Scotch-Brite Never Rust Wool Soap Pads*
1980ʌ	**Jeanne Lee Crews** *space bumper*
1980ʌ	**Karla Sachi** *Space Kids 3000 dolls*
1980ʌ	**Estelle Panzer, Janis Odensky, Judy Jordan** *Tradition (board game: a Jewish version of Trivial Pursuit)*
1980	**Valerie L. Thomas** *illusion transmitter*
1980	**Mildred Smith** *The Family Treedition (board game)*
1982	**Martina Kempf** *voice-controlled wheelchair*